Dropping In On...
COSTA RICA

Patricia M. Moritz

A Geography Series

ROURKE CORPORATION, INC.
VERO BEACH, FLORIDA 32964

Library of Congress Cataloging-In-Publication Data

Moritz, Patricia M.
Costa Rica/Patricia M. Moritz.
p. cm. — (Dropping in on)
Includes index.
Summary: Describes some of the major cities and regions of this small Central American country.
ISBN 0-86593-495-9
1. Costa Rica—Description and travel—Juvenile literature.
[1. Costa Rica—Description and travel.] I. Title.
II. Series.
F1544.M793   1998
917.28604'5—dc21   98-15467
                                CIP
                                AC

Costa Rica

Official Name: The Republic of Costa Rica

Area: 19,730 square miles (51,000 square kilometers)

Population: 3.2 million

Capital: San José

Largest City: San José (pop. 296,300)

Highest Elevation: Cerro Chirripó Grande, 12,526 feet (3,819 meters)

Official Language: Spanish

Major Religion: Roman Catholic

Money: Costa Rican colón

Form of Government: Multiparty democracy

Flag:

TABLE OF CONTENTS

Our Blue Ball—The Earth

The Earth can be divided into two hemispheres. The word hemisphere means "half a ball"—in this case, the ball is the Earth.

The equator is an imaginary line that runs around the middle of the Earth. It separates the Northern Hemisphere from the Southern Hemisphere. North America—where Canada, the United States, and Mexico are located—is in the Northern Hemisphere.

The Northern Hemisphere

When the North Pole is tilted toward the sun, the sun's most powerful rays strike the northern half of the Earth and less sunshine hits the Southern Hemisphere. That is when people in the Northern Hemisphere enjoy summer. When the

North Pole is tilted away from the sun, and the Southern Hemisphere receives the most sunshine, the seasons reverse. Then winter comes to the Northern Hemisphere. Seasons in the Northern Hemisphere and the Southern Hemisphere are always opposite.

Get Ready for Costa Rica

Let's take a trip! Climb into your hot-air balloon, and we'll drop in on a country located on the isthmus of Central America. The Republic of Costa Rica lies between Nicaragua on its northern border and Panama on its eastern border. It is a small country, about the size of Vermont and New Hampshire combined.

There are three mountain ranges, some with active volcanoes. Costa Rica means "rich coast," and it has miles of coastline on two seas. The country forms a bridge between the Pacific Ocean and the Caribbean Sea. Much of Costa Rica's coastal area is covered with dense rain forests.

The government here is stable, and the *ticos*, as Costa Ricans refer to themselves, are proud of their peaceful history. Their constitution forbids them even to have an army.

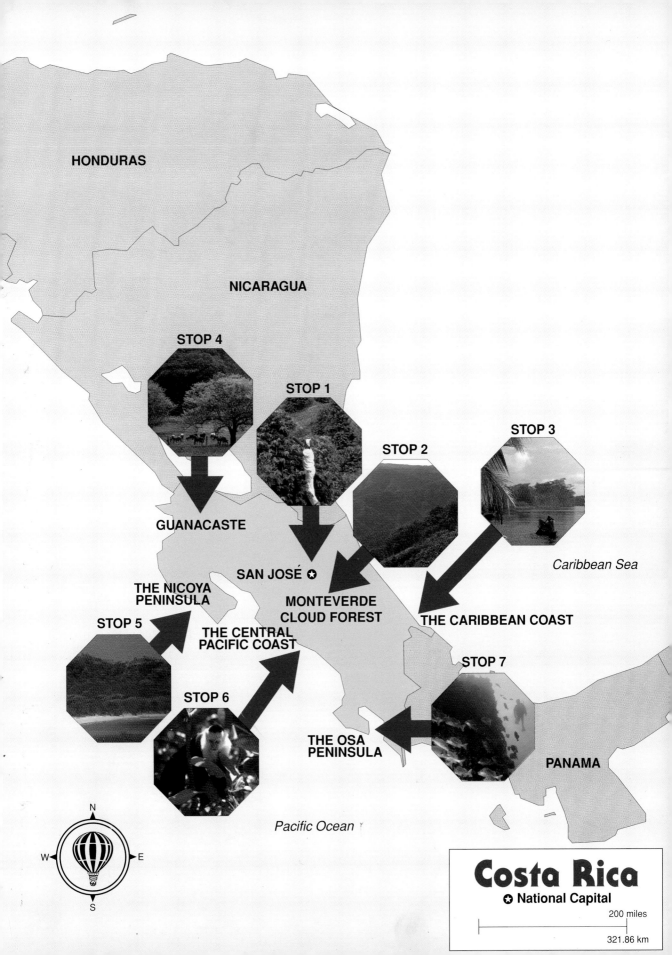

HONDURAS

NICARAGUA

STOP 4

STOP 1

STOP 2

STOP 3

GUANACASTE

SAN JOSÉ ✪

THE NICOYA
PENINSULA

MONTEVERDE
CLOUD FOREST

THE CARIBBEAN COAST

Caribbean Sea

STOP 5

THE CENTRAL
PACIFIC COAST

STOP 6

STOP 7

THE OSA
PENINSULA

PANAMA

Pacific Ocean

N
W · E
S

Costa Rica
✪ National Capital

200 miles

321.86 km

Stop 1: San José

San José is located in the Central Valley of Costa Rica. It is the capital of the country and the most modern city in Central America. The pleasant climate has attracted people from all over the world.

As you walk along you can see the volcanic mountains that surround the city. The mountainsides are covered with coffee plantations. The city was built on the profits of its coffee exports.

One of the most interesting places to visit is The Museo de Entomologia. Here you will see more than one million mounted insects from around the world. There also is a very special butterfly collection. The Serpentarium offers a fascinating look at the many reptile species living in the jungles of Costa Rica, including the numerous poisonous snakes you'll want to avoid.

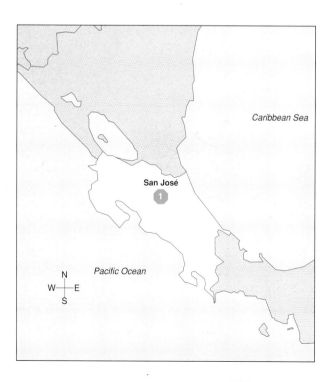

Opposite: A woman picking coffee beans on a plantation near San José.

*Now let's fly **northwest** to the Monteverde Cloud Forest.*

Stop 2: Monteverde Cloud Forest

The Monteverde Biological Cloud Forest Preserve is located in the northern region of Costa Rica. It is a place of great and fragile beauty. Many researchers come here to study the various life forms.

Cloud forests only occur on mountain tops. Moist, warm air sweeps in off the nearby ocean and is forced upward by the mountain slopes. As the moist air rises it cools, forming clouds. All this moisture makes the perfect environment for a variety of plant life. You can see orchids and ferns growing over the branches of huge trees. Nearly every square inch of the forest has some sort of plant growing.

The quetzal bird is the most prized animal living in the cloud forest.

*Now let's fly **east** to the Caribbean coast.*

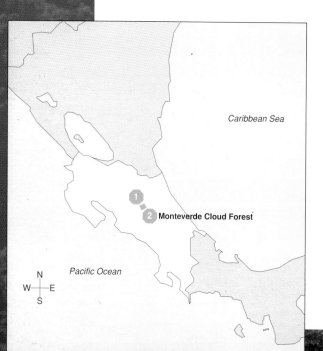

Caribbean Sea

Monteverde Cloud Forest

Pacific Ocean

N
W E
S

Quetzal

Stop 3: The Caribbean Coast

The Caribbean coast of Costa Rica feels very different from the rest of Costa Rica. For a long time this area was so remote that it developed a culture very different from the rest of the country. There is a strong Jamaican influence here. The food is spicier, and the sound of reggae music fills the air.

Tortuguero National Park and Bara del Colorado Wildlife Refuge are located on the northern coast. The main mode of transportation here is by boat on jungle canals.

The major city and only port on this coast is Limón. The biggest event of the year here is the annual Carnival. It is a lively and colorful celebration which lasts about one week.

*Now let's fly **northwest** to Guanacaste.*

Caribbean Sea

Caribbean Coast

Pacific Ocean

N
W—E
S

Volcanoes

Poás, Irazú, and Arenal volcanoes are three of the country's most popular tourist attractions. All three volcanoes lie in the central part of the country.

Irazú last erupted in 1963. The landscape here looks something like the Moon. The views to the Pacific Ocean and the Caribbean Sea are spectacular.

Poás has a crater that measures more than one mile across. It is the second-largest crater in the world. Inside the crater there are geysers which sometimes shoot steam and muddy water 600 feet (182 meters) into the air! A cloud forest rings the crater.

Arenal is Costa Rica's most active volcano. It erupted suddenly and violently in 1968, destroying a nearby village and killing 80 people. The volcano frequently erupts and sends red-hot lava rocks down its western slope. During the day the lava flows steam and rumble.

Opposite: Tabacon volcanic hot springs.

Stop 4: Guanacaste

The Guanacaste province is located in the northwest part of the country. It is Costa Rica's hottest and driest region. Also known as Costa Rica's "Wild West," it is a dry landscape of cattle ranches and cowboys called *sabaneros*.

The most interesting place to visit in this region is Rincon de la Vieja National Park. You will see many sights similar to those found in Yellowstone National Park in the United States. As you hike along the many trails, you can see bubbling mudpots, hot springs, geysers, and volcanic craters.

Hiking to the Blue Lake and La Cangrega Waterfall you will pass through several natural zones from dry forest to open savannah.

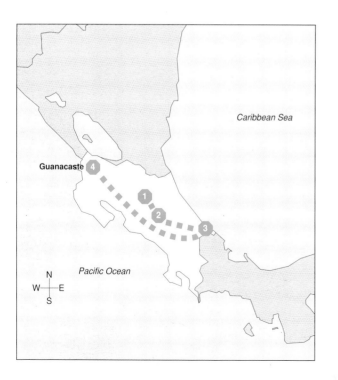

Caribbean Sea

Guanacaste 4

Pacific Ocean

N
W—E
S

*Now let's fly **southward** to the Nicoya Peninsula.*

Stop 5: The Nicoya Peninsula

You'll need a four-wheel drive vehicle to travel the dirt roads into the Nicoya Peninsula.

At the southernmost tip of the peninsula is the Cabo Blanco Absolute Nature Reserve. See howler monkeys as you hike through the lush tropical forest on your way to some of the most beautiful and deserted beaches in the country. At the beach you will see brown pelicans, magnificent frigate birds, and other bird species who nest here.

Nearby is Playa Montezuma, famous for its miles of almost abandoned beaches, rich wildlife, and jungle waterfalls.

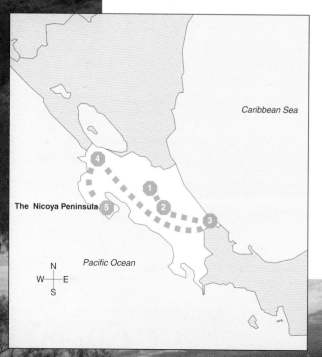

Caribbean Sea

The Nicoya Peninsula

Pacific Ocean

N
W E
S

*Now let's fly **southeast** to the Central Pacific coast.*

Growing Up in Costa Rica

The family is important at all levels of society in Costa Rica. Several generations often live in the same house. Many families make traditional handicrafts to sell in the local markets.

More people in Costa Rica can read and write than in any other Latin American country. Preschool, primary, secondary, and university education are available in Costa Rica. Schools are run by the government or the church. Some plantation owners provide schools for the workers' children. Schools are much better in the towns than in the rural areas.

Education is free, but many children do not go to school. Often children need to work to help provide money for their families. In the cities they sell fruit, wash cars, or polish shoes. In the country they work on the farms.

Soccer and baseball are very popular pastimes with children in Costa Rica.

Stop 6: The Central Pacific Coast

The central Pacific coast is home to some of the most spectacular national parks and animal reserves in the Costa Rica.

The Carara Biological Reserve is a world-renowned nesting ground for scarlet macaws.

Manuel Antonio National Park is the most famous tourist destination in Costa Rica. Here the rain forest meets the blue Pacific Ocean. The beaches are a paradise, and the jungles are crawling with white-faced and squirrel monkeys. You can also see three-toed sloths and purple-and-orange crabs.

Mount Chirripó is the tallest mountain in Costa Rica and one of its great adventures. Backpack through the cloud forest to the summit. Here you can see the Caribbean Sea and Pacific Ocean at the same time.

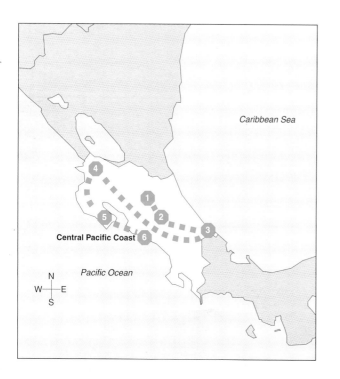

Opposite: A howler monkey at Manuel Antonio National Park.

*Now let's fly **southeast** to the Osa Peninsula.*

Stop 7: The Osa Peninsula

You must be adventurous to explore the southern region of Costa Rica. The most fascinating spots can be reached only by small plane or boat.

The Osa Peninsula has an unbelievable variety of plant and animal life. If you're lucky, you might see an osa, the giant anteaters that live on the peninsula.

The Corcovado National Park located here is well known among naturalists and researchers studying rain forest ecology.

Throughout southern Costa Rica you can see hundreds of mysterious granite spheres left by an ancient civilization. The coral reefs off Canu Island are a great place for a snorkeling or scuba-diving adventure. Hook a world-record marlin or sailfish in the waters off Golfito!

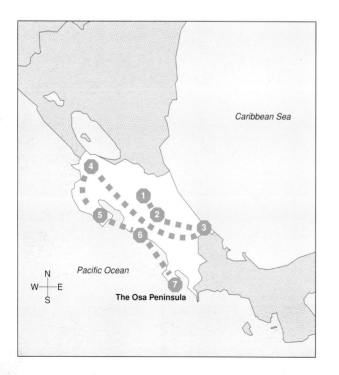

Caribbean Sea

Pacific Ocean

N W E S

The Osa Peninsula

Now its time to set sail for home.

The Foods of Costa Rica

Rice and beans are the center of Costa Rican meals, starting with breakfast. At lunch or dinner, rice and beans are part of a *casado*. It usually is served with cabbage-and-tomato salad, fried plantains (a banana-like vegetable), and a chicken, fish, or meat dish. One of Costa Rica's most popular dishes is black-bean soup. It is typically topped with a poached or boiled egg.

With two coasts, seafood is popular around the country. Sea bass is the most common fish, and it is prepared in a variety of ways. One of the most famous ways it is served is *ceviche*, a marinated fish salad.

Only a few vegetable dishes are found in Costa Rica. *Palmito* is a salad made with hearts of palm, which are considered a delicacy in most places. An entire palm tree must be cut down in order to extract the heart, making palmito expensive, even in Costa Rica where palms are plentiful.

For dessert choose from a wealth of tropical fruits including mangoes, passion fruit, and star fruit.

Glossary

cloud forest   A forest, usually near coastal mountains in tropical regions, that almost always is covered in clouds.

isthmus   A narrow strip of land with water on each side that connects two larger bodies of land.

plantain   A green, tropical banana eaten as a vegetable.

rain forest   A dense, tropical forest that gets heavy rainfall throughout the year.

reggae   A type of popular music originally from Jamaica.

ticos   Native Costa Ricans.

Further Reading

Castello Cortes, Ian. *World Reference Atlas.*
  New York: Dorling Kindersley Limited, 1995.
Greenspan, Eliot. *Frommer's 98: Costa Rica.* Simon
  & Schuster, Inc., 1997.
Palmer, John. *Guide to Places of the World.* New
  York: The Reader's Digest Association, Inc., 1995.
Sawicki, Sandra. *Costa Rica in Pictures.* New York:
  Sterling Publishing Co., 1974.

Suggested Web Sites

Britannica Online
<http://www.info@eb.com>

Knowledge Adventure Encyclopedia
<http://www.adventure.com>

Search engine:
<http:www//yahoo.com>

Index

Acknowledgments and Photo Credits
Cover: Picture Network; pg. 11: João Bittar/Angular/Westlight; pp. 12–13, 19, 20–21, 22, 25: ©Nik
Wheeler/Westlight; pg. 17: ©Peter Horree/Westlight; pg. 23: Ralph Starkweather/Westlight; pg. 27: ©Ralph
Clevenger/Westlight; pg. 29: ©Mike Yamashita/Westlight.
Maps by Paul Calderon.

DATE DUE

FOLLETT